All mimsy were the borogoves,

And the mome raths outgrabe.

"Beware the Jabberwock, my son!
    The jaws that bite, the claws that catch!

"Beware the Jubjub bird, and shun
The frumious Bandersnatch!"

He took his vorpal sword in hand:
  Long time the manxome foe he sought—

So rested he by the Tumtum tree,
And stood awhile in thought.

And, as in uffish thought he stood,
　The Jabberwock, with eyes of flame,
Came whiffling through the tulgey wood,

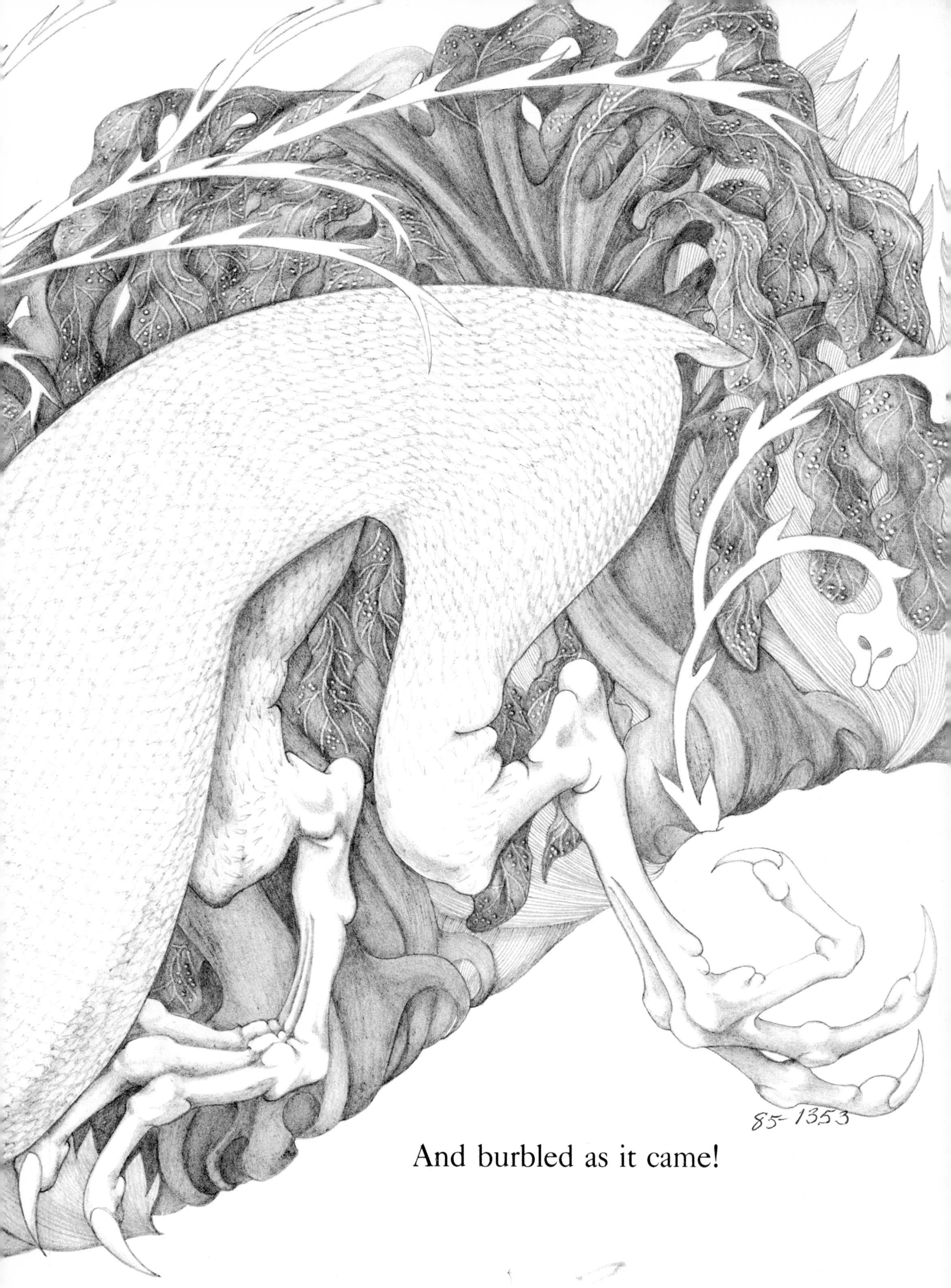

And burbled as it came!

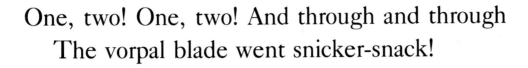

One, two! One, two! And through and through
  The vorpal blade went snicker-snack!

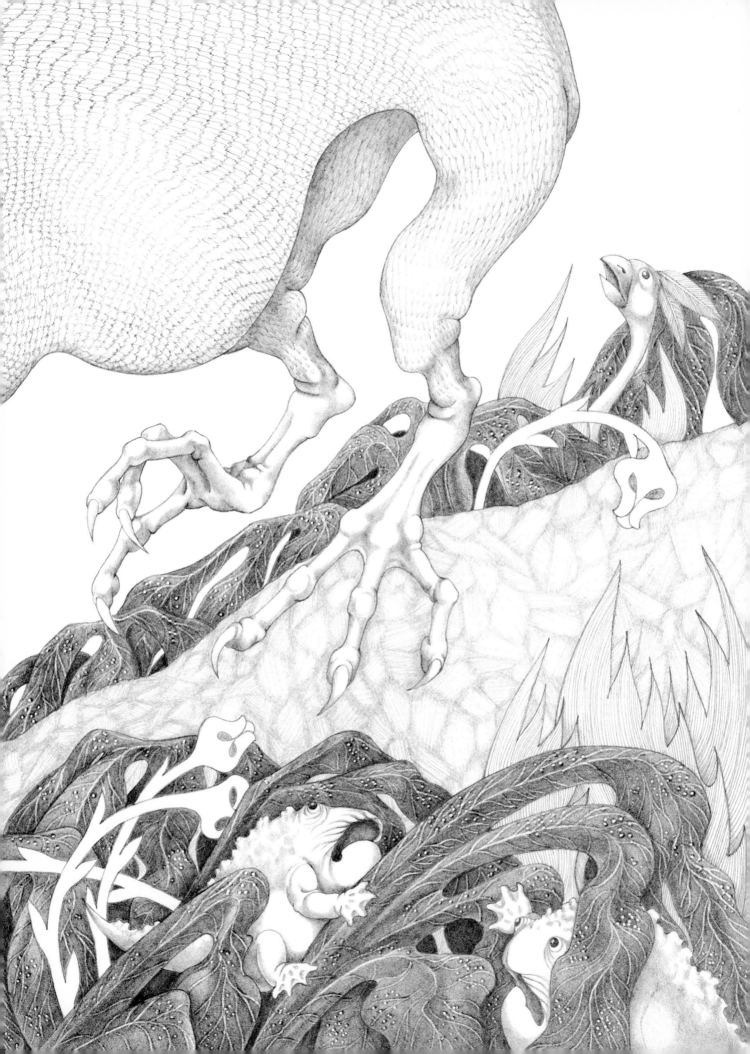

He left it dead, and with its head
He went galumphing back.

"And hast thou slain the Jabberwock?
Come to my arms, my beamish boy!

"O frabjous day! Callooh! Callay!"
He chortled in his joy.

'Twas brillig, and the slithy toves
Did gyre and gimble in the wabe:

All mimsy were the borogoves,
And the mome raths outgrabe.

About Lewis Carroll

Lewis Carroll is the pen name of Charles Dodgson. Dodgson, born in England in 1832, was a teacher of mathematics at Christ Church College of Oxford University and a deacon of the Church of England. He is famous as the author of *Alice in Wonderland* and *Through the Looking Glass*, nonsense stories he began writing to entertain a young friend, Alice Liddell.

"Jabberwocky," from *Through the Looking Glass*, is one of the world's most famous nonsense poems. It is filled with portmanteau words like *slithy*. Humpty Dumpty explains, "Well, '*slithy*' means 'lithe and slimy.' 'Lithe' is the same as 'active.' You see it's like a portmanteau—there are two meanings packed up into one word." But it is not necessary to figure out the meanings of the words in the poem to enjoy it. As Alice herself says, "Somehow it seems to fill my head with ideas—only I don't know exactly what they are."

About Kate Buckley

"It was an honor to collaborate with Lewis Carroll on my first book," says Kate Buckley. Although "Jabberwocky" is often introduced to children when they are in grade school or junior high, she believes the poem can appeal to preschoolers as the story of a little boy who conquers a fearsome beast and wins the approval of his father.

Kate Buckley lives with her husband, children, and cat in Matteson, Illinois, which is as far from Chicago as the commuter trains run south. She obtained a Ph.D. and did post-doctoral research in psychophysiology before turning to children's book writing and illustration. She also teaches statistics at a local university.

Library of Congress Cataloging in Publication Data

Carroll, Lewis, 1832-1898.
    Jabberwocky.

    Summary: The classic nonsense poem taken from "Alice in Wonderland" is illustrated with a father and son in modern dress.
    1. Children's poetry, English.   2. Nonsense verses, English.   [1. Nonsense verse]   I. Buckley, Kate, ill. II. Title.
PR4611.T52 1985   821'.8   84-17339
ISBN 0-8075-3747-0   (lib. bdg.)

Illustrations © 1985 by Kate Buckley
Published in 1985 by Albert Whitman & Company, Niles, Illinois.
Published simultaneously in Canada by General Publishing, Limited, Toronto.
All rights reserved. Printed in the United States of America.
10   9   8   7   6   5   4   3   2   1